HONEY HUNTERS OF NEPAL

ERIC VALLI
DIANE SUMMERS

For Ubs
2015

HARRY N. ABRAMS, INC., PUBLISHERS, NEW YORK

ACKNOWLEDGMENTS:

We thank all those who have helped us to create this book:
His Royal Highness Prince Gyanendra Bir Bikram Shah,
chairman of the King Mahendra Trust, Mr. B. N. Upreti,
director of the Department of National Parks, and Mr. H.
Mishra, secretary of the Wild Life Committee, for their
difficult task in balancing the preservation of nature with
human needs in Nepal; Mani Lal and the hunters, without
whose friendship and patience this book would never have
been made; Monsieur Rietzler, president of Wild-Leitz
(France), Monsieur Yves Maxence, and all the team at Leica
for their generous cooperation; Monsieur Benoît Nacci, art
director of Nathan, for his creativity and enthusiasm in the
making of the book; Elizabeth and Chino, for their friendship and generosity; Lhakpa Gyalzen Sherpa, our assistant
in the field, whose humor never left him even in the most
difficult conditions; and Mr. Ben Underwood, who taught us
more about the bees.

All photographs were taken with Leica R cameras on
Kodachrome professional 64 and 200 film. Only this com-
bination allowed such high-quality enlargements. Most of
the photographs were shot at full aperture because of low
light conditions. The Leica lenses used were: 19mm, 28mm,
35mm, 60mm, 80mm, 90mm, 180mm, 280mm, and dou-
bler. The 80mm lens survived a fall of over one hundred
yards from the top of Samser Bir (photo 14), and we were
able to continue using it, as photographs 26, 27, 28, 56, and
62 testify.

TO MANI LAL AND THE HONEY HUNTERS

Editor, English-language edition: Alexandra Bonfante-Warren
Designer: Benoît Nacci

Library of Congress Cataloging-in-Publication Data
Valli, Éric.
Honey Hunters of Nepal / by Eric Valli and Diane Summers.
p.   cm.
ISBN 0–8109–2408–0 (pbk.)
1. Gurung (Nepalese people) 2. Honey—Nepal.
I. Summers, Diane. II. Title.
DS493.9.G84V35 1988   639—dc19   88–10490CIP

"*Kati mahina pahile shikari-le mahaa tipna ghayo?*" ("How many months ago did the hunters last take the honey?") The old man and his large family sit watching me closely, for the coming of Westerners into their village is a rare event. Counting the creases of his fingers with the tip of his thumb, he recites in English, "October, November, December, January, February, March, April . . . *saat mahina bhayo* (seven months ago)." In this valley deep in the Himalayan foothills of Nepal and several days' walk from the nearest road, it is astonishing that he speaks a word of English. Outside the verandah of his mud-brick house, only the buffalo stir under the hot midday sun. A feeling of timelessness passes over the sleepy village that has been changed little by the passage of the centuries.

"Karma Bahadur, how did you learn English?" The conversation continues in Nepali as he explains, "Oh, when I was in Italy." A gap-toothed smile lights up his wrinkled brown face as he sees my surprise. "In 1933, I left this village with my friend Chitra Bahadur, and we walked to the army recruiting post at the Indian border. We enlisted in the Gurkha regiments of the British Army," he says proudly, "like our fathers did during the First World War. In 1941 we were taken to fight in Persia and Iraq, then on to Egee (Egypt), Elala (El Alamein), Monte Cassino. . . . I speak Italian also . . . *vino!*" he gestures broadly with his hands.

"For forty-five days we were in the desert. Hot by day, cold by night, we fought. We didn't even have a chance to take our shoes off. Our socks were stuck to the soles of our feet; when we returned to camp, the doctor had to cut them away from our skin!" He chuckles as if the pain and discomfort meant nothing to him. "We fought in some of the biggest battles. At Monte Cassino we slept in bomb craters with bombardments all around. Our friends died but we didn't meet death." Of the seven boys who left the village to fight during the Second World War, four returned. Known as the "pension wallahs," the survivors are regarded as men of standing in their communities. The modest army pensions make them comfortably off in comparison with their neighbors, who can only feed their families. Tales of combat in far-off places and medals proving their bravery give them the high status that elected Karma as headman.

The young men of Karma's ethnic group, the Gurungs, continue to be recruited to the Gurkha regiments of the British and Indian armies. Although they fight for countries other than their own, their reputation as courageous soldiers is untouched by any pejorative connotations of the word "mercenary." For a Gurung boy, the Gurkhas offer an opportunity to travel, a good salary, and a chance to win prestige in his village. But despite the attractive conditions of army life, most return after serving out their contracts of around sixteen years. For them, the pure air and beauty of their mountain homeland are far better than the life in the malaria-ridden valleys and plains to the south. They resume the lives of farmers and, with the money saved from their pay and pensions, buy land and build a house.

The Gurungs live along the southern slopes of the Himalayas in west-central Nepal. Soaring over twenty-six thousand feet into a deep blue sky, the highest mountain range of the world dominates the clusters of ocher houses clinging to its steep hillsides. Every possible slope has been wrested from the earth for cultivation, carved into terraces often as high as they are wide. Those few too precipitous retain the last stands of the forest that once covered the valleys. Paths worn by decades of porters and local people wind past emerald-green tiers of young corn and through the villages. Beyond the mountain region, the hazy blue lines of valleys and ridges extend southward, gradually melting into the Gangetic plain of northern India.

The morning sun rises late above the ridges, illuminating the blue shadows with the colors of the day. A woman, clad in a cotton sari and resting a copper urn on her hip, walks slowly to the village fountain. She stops to fill the container with water and to gossip with the women beating the dirt from their washing. A boy passes, urging the three buffalo in his charge along a narrow trail. The clucking of chickens, the pounding of rice, and the sifting of chaff from the grain fill the air.

Karma Bahadur's neighbor Mani Lal gathers a few possessions for a hunting trip. Born sixty-three years ago, his destiny was to be neither a Gurkha soldier nor a farmer. Having inherited insufficient land to feed his family, Mani Lal tried to join the Gurkhas but failed to pass the physical examination. Following the tradition of his father and forefathers, he became a hunter of game and honey. "Since my childhood," Mani Lal explains, "I've preferred running in the forest to mixing dung with earth. And so I became a hunter, a man of the forest like my ancestors."

The Gurungs were once hunters and gatherers. Gradually they settled and turned to terraced crop cultivation. They set a pattern for future generations as they went to work clearing the forests for fields, stripping the trees for fodder, and cutting the timber for firewood. As the population grows, the forests continue to shrink, and villages are surrounded by widening circles of denuded hillsides scarred by erosion. With the loss of agricultural productivity through ecological decline and the diminution of plots through the division of land by inheritance, more villagers must sell their farms or go into debt. Fortunate are those with a son in the army to send a regular salary. For the hunters, honey and wax are vital economic assets that are sold or traded for food.

Mani Lal does not walk with Karma's military bearing, but with the agility and suppleness of a youth. Small and lithe, he passes through the low doorway of his house, filling a bag with millet flour. He has put a handful of chilis, a pouch of tobacco, and a bamboo water pipe into his shoulder bag, and taken down an old musket from the wall. His slight build might lead an observer to underestimate his strength. His almond-shaped eyes, sharp and penetrating, his high cheekbones, and slightly flattened nose reveal the Mongol origins of his tribe. His firm chin, covered with white stubble, denotes a strong will, just as his reserved and blunt nature reflects a man more at ease in nature than in the company of strangers. The last time he visited Kathmandu, six days from his village, was fifteen years ago. The capital of Nepal holds no interest for Mani Lal; he prefers to hunt in the jungle.

Mani Lal and the other eight hunters from his village leave after the May full-moon festivities celebrating Buddha's birth. The Gurungs follow their own blend of Hinduism and Buddhism, the two major religions of Nepal. They observe the major festivals of each, but the Buddhist precept against killing does not prevent them from performing sacrifices. Their priests are lamas who have studied in the Tibetan monasteries of Kathmandu, but it is the astrologer from the Hindu caste of Brahmins who is called upon to read the chart of a newly born infant or study the compatibility of a couple before a betrothal is made. Also powerful in their lives are the local protective and malevolent spirits living in the jungle, rocks, and rivers. It falls to the village shaman to exorcise a spirit causing illness or misfortune from an afflicted house or person.

Before crossing the first river, Mani Lal waits for his companions to arrive. He shuts his eyes and feels the warmth of the sun through the thin fabric of his shirt, gray and worn with the months of constant wear. Sri Lal, his younger brother by eight years, is the first to join him. Without saying a word, Sri Lal lights a cigarette and, holding it between fingers curled tight into a fist, draws deeply a few times before passing it to Mani Lal. Sri Lal's eccentric

The earliest evidence of the relation between human beings and bees is this rock painting from the Spider Cave, near Valencia, Spain. The painting testifies to 12,000 years of honey hunting.

and gruff nature has made him the most solitary of the hunters. Timid at heart, yet bustling with energy, he absorbs himself in cooking, filtering the honey, and processing the wax. Bal Bahadur, at forty-seven years old the youngest brother, strides up the trail wearing shoes and bright red socks bought in Kathmandu. Sri Lal looks at his own bare feet and then at his little brother's shoes. "Are they made from the same leather as bus seats?" he asks. Bal Bahadur laughs. His occasional trips to the government offices of Kathmandu as mayor of the village and possession of the only radio in the valley have made him sophisticated and worldly in comparison with his brothers. He is the only one of the hunters who is literate; as the group's accountant, he measures the honey yield and calculates the share of each hunter. Mani Lal and Sri Lal are as quick-tempered and direct as their brother is polite and courteous. Sri Lal growls like a bear and complains that the six others are late.

Akam, Krishna Bahadur, Nanda Lal, Amarzang, and Purké arrive together. Each carries a *dokko*, a woven bamboo basket, containing cooking pots, bags of flour, and large tin containers for the honey. All goods are transported on people's backs along the network of paths that connect villages in Nepal. Cigarettes are taken out of the folds of their waistbands and shared around.

"We leave for about twenty suns," says Mani Lal, chief of the group. "Bal Bahadur went up to the lower reaches of the gorge and saw five big nests. We will begin there and work our way up the gorge and then over the ridge to the next valley." Men Bahadur, tall and muscular, slowly walks toward the others and lowers the large circular roll of the bamboo ladder from his back and onto a boulder. He wipes the sweat from his brow and takes the proffered half of a burning cigarette. "Our family is now all here," continues Mani Lal. "Tonight we make camp where the two rivers meet. Tomorrow morning, after the sacrifice, we will begin work."

Mani Lal rules the world of the honey hunters. He decides the dates of the hunt, distributes the tasks, the meat, and the honey. None of his orders are ever discussed. He guides the hunters along invisible trails that dissect the forest. He is the only one able to speak with the gods and to descend the ladder.

"No one can remember how long we have been eating the honey of the cliffs," says Mani Lal. "Our families have been honey hunters for a very long time. My father, Barta, initiated me into the secrets of taking the honey and the sacred *mantras* that appease the gods. He was taught by his uncles, who learned from their father, Barchi. He followed the work of Chitra Bahadur who fell to his death on the cliffs." Although no earliest date has been put on the honey hunting of the Gurungs, cave paintings discovered in Spain, South Africa, and India show remarkable similarities to the methods of Mani Lal and the hunters; reaching back some twelve thousand years to the end of the Paleolithic period, they testify to a long history.

Generation after generation of hunters have passed down the skills of the honey harvest to their sons. Nanda Lal, who presses the wax; Men Bahadur, who carries the ladder; Amarzang, who holds the ropes; Akam and Krishna, who light the fires; each of them learned from his father. If a hunter's son is not able or willing to take up his father's work, the training is passed to a nephew or cousin. But it is always Mani Lal who has final say over the choice of a successor. "It is important that we are one"—the old man interlocks his fingers tightly—"otherwise, if one is not

happy he can easily push us from the mountain."

Mani Lal's village is the last human habitation before the forest begins at the junction of two mountain torrents. This is the border separating the cultivated valleys of man from the sacred domain of Pholo, god of the jungle, the cliffs, and the hunt. Mani Lal withdraws from the group and gathers a small bundle of branches. In a low voice, he recites *mantras* of protection and taps each of the hunters on the shoulder with the branches. He places them under a stone in the middle of the path to prevent any village witches from following them across the river.

Mani Lal leads his men on faint trails that meander ever deeper into the forest. He carries only two long bamboo poles that bang on the rocks and ground behind him. Akam, fifty-one, follows. He is one of Mani Lal's oldest friends. An orphan without land, he has never married. Shy and introverted, he works quietly, lighting the fires to smoke the bees from their nests. Krishna, thirty-nine, is the smallest but his body is hard and muscular. He climbs the narrow cliff edges with the nimbleness of a monkey to light the fires close to the nests. Nanda Lal, forty-two, comes next. He wears the black waistcoat of a city shopkeeper over his shirt woven from nettles, and sports canvas shoes on his feet. Like Bal Bahadur, he bought these luxuries on a trip to "Nepal," as the Gurung villagers call Kathmandu. But unlike the mayor's, Nanda Lal's clothes are in stark contrast to his poverty. Amarzang is, at thirty-eight years old, the youngest of them all. Although he is the lighthearted one of the group, his task is the most difficult, after the old man's. He is Mani Lal's assistant and remains close to him on the cliff, maneuvering on tiny ledges without the security of a rope. Purké is the oldest; although he has retired from the hunt, he accompanies the hunters occasionally to help around the camp. Men Bahadur closes the file. He walks slowly, carrying the 160-foot-long ladder made from the cortex of mountain bamboo, wound in a seventy-seven-pound coil on his back. Only the calves of his legs and his broad feet are visible. Although tall for a Gurung and the strongest of all the hunters, he has a simple and gentle nature.

Like creatures of the forest, the nine men blend in with their environment: their felted woolen capes, or *bokkus*, are the color of dead leaves; their legs, like tree trunks, are strong and sinewy; their knees are like the wrinkled knots of old trees; their bare, gnarly feet, like spreading roots, grip the earth. Sleek calf muscles ripple under copper skin. Naked feet take the shape of the rocks and earth, leaving the imprints of spreading toes in the mud. Unhesitatingly they jump from stone to stone across a torrent with the gracefulness of deer. From time to time they stop to pick the leeches off their feet and legs. Men Bahadur spits tobacco juice on his feet to repel the bloodsuckers.

Under the shelter of an overhanging rock, the hunters make camp. The smoke of the fire marks the only human presence in the primeval forest. Their voices are drowned by the roar of the torrent, as ever-present as the crashing of the waves by the sea.

In the early morning, before the sun touches the gorge, Mani Lal shapes the figure of the jungle god from a thick millet paste. On a stone slab he places the effigy and offerings: an egg; handfuls of rice, millet, and popcorn; a strand of sheep's wool; and juniper. He carries the stone to the side of the river. Men Bahadur follows

with a plump chicken in his hands. Squatting on a boulder, Mani Lal murmurs incantations to Pholo. He sprinkles the corn over the slab and burns the juniper. A sweet, acrid smoke rises. The chicken struggles in Men's hands as if sensing its impending fate. Three times Mani Lal sprinkles water over the chicken to purify it for the sacrifice. Holding a long, curved knife between his knees, Mani Lal neatly slices its throat over the blade. Facing the jungle, Mani Lal addresses the god: "Pholo, I give this sacrifice of blood to you. Now that I have offered you blood, please do not take any of our lives." As the hunt is in Pholo's domain and for his creatures, the hunters will not begin their campaign until the sacrifice is made. Failure to make offerings would offend the god, and the hunters believe that they would risk misfortune, ill health, or even death. Mani Lal remembers well the story of his father:

> Thirty years before, Barta was a honey hunter as I am now. One day, at the beginning of the hunt, he made the *puja* to Pholo. But he did not do it with a good heart. He thought, "My ancestors made the sacrifice, but I don't believe in this god. He is just a story of the old people." After the fires were lit to smoke away the bees, Barta climbed down the ladder and began to cut down the nest. Because the *puja* was not made with a strong belief, the bees attacked. Thousands covered him. A pain like a knife seared through his eye; he was blinded by a sting. He never regained his sight. He did not know that Pholo was a great god—he made the mistake. That is how I inherited the tradition of my father and became a honey hunter.

Mani Lal returns to the camp carrying the slab. He cracks open the egg and carefully examines its color and consistency to determine if someone will fall ill and when the hunt will finish. He turns the chicken over the flames and plucks off the feathers. Tearing open the chest, he carefully examines the lungs for omens.

Mani Lal reads the lungs of a sacrificed chicken like a book of divination. White or red marks, horizontal or vertical lines, all foretell future events. A white vein pointing upwards from the center indicates certain death, but the presence of red lines means there is some hope. These lungs, however, have no imperfections; the hunters can enter the new venture without risk. The swelling like a small head is an excellent omen for a bountiful hunt.

Sri Lal cooks a chicken curry. Not a single morsel is wasted: bones, flesh, and skin all go into the cooking pot. A cauldron of *deero*—the thick porridge that is a staple of the Gurung diet—bubbles on the fire. The long bamboo water pipe gurgles. Mani Lal taps the clay cone to empty out the ashes. "It's thirty years old now; I traded a measure of honey for it on the birth of my first daughter." He fills the cone with several pinches of thickly cut tobacco and on top places a live coal from the fire. Resting his mouth over the opening of the hookah, he draws deeply in a concert of gurgles. He savors the smoke, then draws again before passing it to the next man.

Sri Lal shares out dollops of *deero* onto leaves the size of a hand. He reapportions a little from one leaf to the next to ensure that the servings are exactly even, then tops each with a bright red chili. "Salt is our *pranayama* (breath), but chili is the taste!" he exclaims. Each of the hunters places a small ball of the paste from his plate onto a stone of the hearth as an offering to Pholo. Only then do they begin eating, for the gods must always be provided for first. They roll the *deero* into balls and dip them into the chicken curry. No one talks until the plates are wiped clean. Belches confirm that the meal was good.

The hunters leave for Kyumro Bir, the stepped cliff of rocks and nests. All of the cliffs have names: Samser Bir (The Cliff of Three Hundred Nests), Kirlu (From a Small Nest Comes a Lot of Honey), and Sabro (Scattered Bees' Nests). Purké, too old for the difficult trail ahead, stays at the camp. The line of brown-hooded figures threads silently through the virgin forest. Nimbly they climb a slippery trail scented with the fecund blend of decaying leaves and dark loamy soil. Birds twitter in the tall trees. Sunlight filters through the broad canopy, casting a dappled golden light. The path turns steeply up the wall of the gorge and disappears into thick tangles of nettle and bracken. Mani Lal swings up and over a low-hanging branch to reach the higher trail. None of the others can follow this sixty-three-year-old man; instead they cut through the undergrowth with sickles.

At the junction of the hunters' trail and a path from the village, a party of boys and men awaits. All wear *bokkus* as protection against the bees and carry a variety of containers in anticipation of collecting the honey. Although they come to take and not to work, they are welcomed by the hunters. Every year a tax of five hundred rupees (twenty-five dollars) is levied by the Nepalese government on the hunt, whether or not any honey is found. The hunters never know what the yield will be. If there is little or no honey to pay the levy, the equivalent of four cents is collected from each villager, who then has the right to take some of the honey at the next harvest. The villages are large, and in this way the hunters have enough to pay the tax.

The jungle path snakes deeper through dense foliage, disappearing between tall trees, their thick branches veiled with strands of lichen. Mani Lal continues to lead the way, for he is the only one who knows the way to the cliffs. "Mani Lal would know how to follow the scent of a deer," Amarzang jokes. Ferns growing to chest height, thick vines, and bushes hide the ground where the walkers must place their bare feet. The leeches that have appeared with the first rains waver their heads towards the warm bodies. Akam slips; Krishna helps him to his feet and to hoist the *dokko* onto his back again. The ladder is the biggest and most awkward load. It catches the lianas, ferns, and bamboos. Under the lowest branches, Men Bahadur advances on his knees. Despite all the hindrances, he walks without anger or complaint, his eyes lost in a dream. The line of hunters and villagers stops at the foot of a rocky passage. Mani Lal and Amarzang, the most agile, climb up; the loads are then passed from hand to hand to the top. Rarely are words exchanged, yet the hunters are an efficient team. Each man has great respect for his companions. They all know that if one breaks his leg or is attacked by a bear, there is little chance of survival alone. "Like the many fibers woven together to make the long, strong rope, our hands, our forces, are united to allow us to go where one man could never travel," says Mani Lal, adding, "but the bee is a better example of solidarity than man." A strange rapport exists between the old man and the bees. He feels a mixture of admiration for their society, greed for the honey, and fear of their attacks. Mani Lal points to the large black crescent high on the cliff face. At first glance it looks like a rock, but suddenly the surface ripples. Thousands of bees are clustered together on the comb. "We have done the *puja*, paid

the tax, now I will take the honey," he says.

The villagers and the hunters responsible for lighting the fires and filtering the honey take a lower trail for the base of the cliff. "Be quiet when you get close to the cliff," warns Mani Lal, "or else the bees will know that we're here and will attack." He leads Men Bahadur and Amarzang to the top of the cliff; they pull themselves upward with the stands of bamboo, finding their footing on tree roots and stones. At the top, Men Bahadur unrolls the ladder over the edge of the cliff. The ladder has a beautiful golden color, having spent the winter over Akam's hearth. The smoke keeps the insects off and protects it from rotting, but the fibers dry out, rendering it fragile. At the camp the ladder is soaked in water and carefully checked, for Mani Lal's life depends on its strength.

Men Bahadur ties the ladder around the base of a tree trunk and holds the ropes firmly. Because of his strength, he has the job of moving the ladder in the directions commanded by Mani Lal. Amarzang, the first to go down, takes his post on a lip of the cliff close to the nest. Mani Lal sits on the edge of the void, a drop of more than 150 feet into the gorge. Up here, sheltered by the overhanging cliff, the roar of the torrent is inaudible. The only sounds are the calls of birds, the rustle of leaves, and the whisper of the wind. Mani Lal takes a small pouch of rice from his waistband and empties it into a broad leaf. Reciting the different names of Pholo, he sprinkles the grains in the air. "There have been one death and one injury on the cliff in my father's time," he reflects. "It was not because a rope fell; it was the god who caused the man to disappear. I must not cut the nest when the god is not pleased. I must always pray first."

Mani Lal puts on his only protection against the bees: a pair of army pants given to him by a cousin in the Gurkhas, and a thick cape. He checks the strings tied around the two bamboo poles and places his arms through the loops. His eyes, usually alert to the slightest movements in the jungle, no longer notice the outside world. His attention has turned inward. Without throwing a glance or saying a word to his companions, Mani Lal starts down the ladder. It creaks under his weight; the knots tighten.

The old man climbs down the swaying ladder like a spider spinning its descent on a frail strand of web. The slightest error of judgment means death. His bare feet hook each rung like the claws of an eagle; his fingers run down the sides of the ladder at the same rhythm. Amarzang watches from his perch. Gripping the ladder with one hand, he leans over the cliff edge, into the dizzying emptiness. The river is a white, snaking line growling as if all the melted snow of the Himalayas was flowing through the narrow chasm. At the foot of the cliff, the tiny pinpricks of heads move around like ants, busily feeding the fire with branches and leaves.

Mani Lal stops beneath an overhang and faces the circular nest almost as big as himself. The thick upper part glued to the rock contains the honey. The lower crescent is the brood comb, made up of thousands of nursery cells containing the bee pupae and larvae. The surface ripples and hums, then falls as still as the surrounding rock. The colony is still covered with bees: the wind is blowing the smoke away from the cliff. Mani Lal gestures a silent order to Amarzang, for he does not want to alert the insects to his presence. In precise teamwork, Amarzang relays the message to Men Bahadur on top of the cliff. Within minutes a flaming bundle of leaves is lowered, and Mani Lal pushes it under the nest with a bamboo. Panic runs over the living surface. The bees buzz furiously and depart in a deafening swarm.

Slowly the golden crescent is unveiled.

"*Uyer!*" Mani Lal cries. Amarzang echoes the message. Men Bahadur throws down a short stick tied to a long rope. The old man threads it through the comb patterned with thousands of hexagonal nursery cells. He then thrusts a bamboo pole along the lower edge of the honeycomb. Nothing distracts him from his task, neither the void below his feet nor the bees crawling over his skin and buzzing around his head. The brood comb breaks from the nest; secured by the rope, it spins and knocks against Mani Lal. The ladder recoils and swings. The hunter holds on tightly until it steadies. "*Hye!*" he shouts. Men Bahadur lowers the comb to the bottom of the cliff. Mani Lal, suspended on the ladder over a 160-foot drop, smokes a cigarette as he waits for the basket to arrive.

Akam grabs the wax crescent as soon as it is within reach and lays it aside. At the end of the day it will be carried back to camp to be cleaned and melted into bricks. The bees buzz furiously around the hunters and villagers. They dart toward the people's faces and, alighting on any exposed skin, curve their abdomens downward to thrust in the stings. *Apis laboriosa* is one of the most aggressive bees in the world: when disturbed, it will attack any moving creature. Angry swarms have been known to attack people as far away as the villages. Krishna, deep inside his *bokku*, feeds leafy branches onto the fire to keep the bees away. The hunters stand close to the smoke; the villagers huddle under their capes for protection.

"*Dalo po ko!*" ("Send the basket!") Mani Lal shouts. Nanda Lal ties a bamboo basket lined with the skin of a wild goat to the rope and, with the relay of messages from the bottom of the cliff to the top, Men Bahadur hauls it up to the level of the colony. Bees crawl over Mani Lal's face and into his hood. He has built up a resistance to the stings and simply picks the bees off before starting to cut down the honeycomb.

Every limb of the old man's body is tensed and at work. He wedges the basket with a bamboo maneuvered by his left leg, while the right foot grips the rung for balance. His two arms thrust the second bamboo pole into the upper part of the nest, gradually peeling off slabs of honeycomb from the rock. Honey runs like molasses, and the comb, heavy with the golden liquid, falls into the basket.

Mani Lal releases the basket, now laden with fifty pounds of honey, from under the nest. The ladder and the basket sway like two pendulums, and the hunter is hit several times with his load of booty. The momentum gradually subsides and finally stops. Mani Lal catches his breath and orders the basket to be lowered.

"It's raining honey!" At the foot of the cliff, the faces of the villagers, smeared with honey and radiant with excitement, turn upward, mouths wide open to catch the golden drops. Bare, sticky arms holding a variety of plates, bowls, and saucepans come from every direction to catch the honey dripping from the nest.

Before the basket touches the ground, the hands of the villagers swoop onto the prize, breaking off chunks of the comb. Sri Lal wrests the basket away and throws the contents into a bamboo filter. Elbow-deep in honey, he quickly presses the mixture of bees, honeycomb, and liquid through the filter and into a copper cauldron. The locals dip their bowls into the filter and, exclaiming excitedly, haggle Sri Lal to fill their pots.

Thunder rumbles and the jungle darkens like a tomb. Large raindrops patter on the leaves. The villagers pull their *bokkus* over their heads, take their bottles and pots filled with honey, and disappear through the trees, their brown forms blending into the colors of the forest. After spending more than one hour on the ladder, Mani Lal descends. The harvest is good: two 60-pound containers are filled and stoppered with pieces of wax. *Apis laboriosa* is well known for its high honey yield, and one large nest can give between 125 and 160 pounds. However, unknowingly, the hunters have become terrible predators. Entire colonies of bees are destroyed when Mani Lal cuts down their nests. If the queen and enough worker bees escape and return, the colony can be quickly reconstructed and, within a month, the nest can be sufficiently pregnant with honey for another expedition to be launched. Careful exploitation would allow the nests to be tapped more efficiently, but the hunters know only the methods of their fathers. The destruction of existing nests and the diminishing forest continue to deplete their numbers each year. "My grandfather would take 1,200 nests in a year," says Mani Lal. "Last year we took 120. This year, perhaps 90. On Samser Bir, the cliff of 300 nests, there are today 15. Now there are not as many bees and nests. In my father's time, our village was jungle. Now it is fields and houses and we have to walk two hours to collect firewood. Many bees have left."

Mani Lal pours a little honey into the palm of his hand and examines the color. It is golden—a sign, the hunters say, that the nest is new. Black honey comes from a nest several months old, they say, while red honey would indicate that the bees had fed on a dead animal. Mani Lal announces that the honey is not *laagne* (toxic), for his palm does not tingle. Even so, he never eats the honey during the hunt, especially before the monsoon, for fear of being poisoned. The hunter's explanation of the *laagne* honey is simple: the bees sometimes collect nectar from poisonous flowers. Before the rains, the poison collects with the nectar, and the honey becomes *laagne*. After the monsoonal rains "wash" the poison from the flowers, the nectar is uncontaminated—the honey will be good.

Occasionally villagers too impatient to wait for Mani Lal's verdict eat the toxic honey. Before they can reach the village, they have collapsed on the jungle path, unable to walk and suffering from cold sweats, vomiting, and impaired vision. There they remain until they can manage to stagger home. Symptoms can last up to several hours, although Mani Lal knows a *mantra* to cure the affliction. Thunder rumbles again: "*Guruuung!*" says Mani Lal, imitating the menacing sound. "We must hurry, otherwise the rain will bite us."

In the late afternoon the hunters sit bare-chested close to the fire, their clothes drying on a branch above their heads. Sri Lal, in nothing but a loincloth from which his long skinny legs jut, looks like a wild man of the jungle. He squeezes the white fluid from the larvae into a small pot of heated honey. Rich in protein, the mixture, considered to be a tonic, is shared among the hunters. Each of them contributes a cup of flour to the cauldron of boiling water. Sri Lal stirs the *deero* with a wooden spatula carved from a branch. Amarzang arrives with a bag of wild mushrooms and fresh nettles. "Tonight we will have nettle soup and fried mushrooms. But there are no little gold ones to send us to the movies!" he laughs. Five years ago, Amarzang saw a movie for the first time when he was in Kathmandu, an experience

he can compare only to the effects of the hallucinogenic mushrooms found in the forest.

Around the fire, the hookah gurgles as it passes from hand to hand. Bamboos click as the hunters weave *dokkos*. Mani Lal takes the tweezers hanging around his neck and pulls the bee stings from his arms. He points to the swollen faces of the others and laughs. "I am old, my flesh is dry and no longer swells. But the flesh of young men is soft and blows up with the bites of bees." Silver streaks of rain dart through the leafy canopy. The cliffs rise steeply into slate-gray skies. The rain falls as if it will never stop, bringing rejuvenation to the forest that is essential to the lives of the hunters. "We are people of the jungle," reflects Mani Lal, "it provides us with what we need. The bamboo is our iron. We weave it to make baskets, the roofs of our houses, and the ladder and ropes of the hunt. Our clothes are made of nettle fiber. When we hunt, our bed is made of leaves, our shelter is our *bokku*, and our food is the fruit of the jungle. We are happy if we have money, but we're just as happy if we don't." He continues:

Our ancestors came from these jungles. It is the legend of our people. A long, long time ago, two brothers came from the north [Mongolia] where the winters were hard, searching for land. They crossed the Himalayas, and came to a deep forest where they lost their way. The

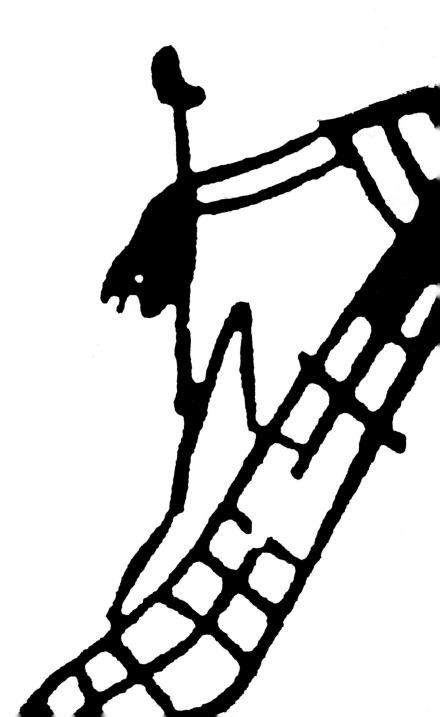

Gathering wild honey in
Natal, South Africa.
Sketch of a rock
carving, after H. Pager.

houettes of trees and bushes. Amarzang recounts his dream
of making love; the others are pleased, for it is a good omen
for the hunt.

Today, Tuesday, an inauspicious day for construct-
ing a roof or harvesting honey, is favorable for
hunting. Mani Lal, Krishna, and Men Bahadur
prepare the old percussion muskets passed down
from their grandfathers. They muzzle-load them
with "three fingers" of black powder and stone bullets. They
place percussion caps on the nipples.

The hunters leave the trails of man for those of wild
animals. Here, there are no human traces. The footprints of
the hunters have been erased by snow, rain, or the tracks of
deer and bear. They walk with the silent suppleness of cats.
Mani Lal gestures to Krishna and Men Bahadur to go in two
different directions. The old man crouches behind boulders
on top of a ridge. Krishna makes a long detour to take up a
position opposite him. Men Bahadur closes the cul-de-sac
trap they have formed. He hides himself in a tree and,
camouflaged by his *bokku*, melts into the leaves.

The gurgling of a stream and the rustle of a falling leaf
are the only sounds to disturb the silence. One hour, two
hours pass. Men Bahadur remains immobile. Only his eyes
are animated as he scrutinizes the thick vegetation. The
cries of their companions grow more distinct as they draw
closer, beating the bushes to frighten the animals into the
trap. The forest wakes up, birds fly away. Slowly Men
Bahadur lowers his gun and pulls the hammer. The shouts
are clearer and louder. A gun thunders to his right. In a
concert of breaking branches, a deer breaks through the
curtain of vines. Men Bahadur fires his gun. An acrid smoke
surrounds the hunter who, had his cape not fallen to the
ground, would seem not to have moved. The shouting stops.
Quiet returns to the forest. Killed instantly, the deer lies on
its side. Blood runs down from a hole behind its shoulder.
Men Bahadur places his hand on its body in a token of
respect.

The hunters believe that no perfect animal falls into their
trap. Only those with a deformity, like a broken hoof or a
blind eye, or those who are too old to run, are given by Pholo.
As soon as an animal is killed, an offering must be made to
the god. Every evening he counts his creatures. He accepts a
death if offerings have been left. If there are no offerings, the
god searches for the beast until he discovers the hunters. He
kills them and gives back life to the animal. "Several years
ago," the hunters recount, "a villager killed a wild goat, but
he gave nothing to Pholo. After eating the meat he fell asleep.
He never awoke."

Men Bahadur slices off the tip of the nose, tongue, ears,
and hooves of the deer. Placing them in a leaf, he addresses
Pholo: "O you, god of the jungle, I took the life of one of your

elder went first, cutting a trail through wild banana
trees. The younger brother was tired and fell asleep.
When he awoke two hours later, he saw that the banana
trees cut by his brother had already grown by a couple
of inches. He didn't know that they grow very quickly.
He thought that he had slept for several days and,
believing that he would have no chance of catching up
with his brother, stayed in the jungle. That is how the
Gurungs began. His elder brother continued walking
and became the father of the Naga tribe in the south.

As night falls, the rain stops. A cloud of mist envelops the
camp, tiny amidst the giant trees. The hunters spread out
their *bokkus* as mattresses, unravel their waistbands as
coverings, and arrange the bags of flour for their pillows. All
night long, Mani Lal wakes and adds branches to the fire to
keep warm.

When the darkness of night turns to gray, a chorus of
birds hidden in the trees brings the first hint of daybreak.
The hunters slowly waken, opening their eyes to the sil-

creatures. Please don't be angry, take some of it first." He kneels down and puts the leaf at the foot of a tree. "But look at this animal, his feet were not good enough to run away from me. One of his ears was torn. It was not a good animal, so I took its life. Thank you for offering it to me."

The hunter ties the legs together with a vine and hoists the deer onto his back. He and his companions return to camp where they skin and cut the animal into pieces. The liver is offered to Pholo. Mani Lal shares out the meat. Men Bahadur receives a leg as he owns the gun that killed it. "There were two deer," says Krishna, "but Mani Lal missed, and the other escaped." A voice whispers, "Before, Mani Lal was the best at the hunt, but now that he is old, he is worthless." Mani Lal overhears but says nothing. Sri Lal jumps to his brother's defense: "He is old, but would any of you go down the ladder to take the honey?" After a long silence Mani Lal speaks: "It's true, I am old. My eyes can no longer see well. But it was my father who taught me how to

cut the honey, and it was his father who taught him. Now that I know everything, I must pass the teaching on to my sons. But none of them wants to be a hunter. They prefer to stay in the village."

Only after twenty-two suns does Mani Lal decide to end the campaign. The hunters have harvested forty colonies. Others remain, but they are not touched, for they are the "seeds" from which those that were destroyed will be rebuilt. Bal Bahadur distributes the honey according to the role of each hunter. Mani Lal keeps the four biggest nests. Bal Bahadur, as mayor and accountant, receives the next largest share. The size of the allotments then diminishes with the level of difficulty of each man's task: Amarzang and Men Bahadur take the same amount, then Krishna and Akam, who tend the fires, and finally Sri Lal and Nanda Lal, who filter the honey and wax. A token amount is reserved for Purké. The honey, which is valued as a universal remedy and tonic, is sold to villagers or exchanged for grain, yogurt,

milk, a chicken, or even a day's work. The price of a pound is ten rupees, the equivalent of fifty cents, a luxury in a country where some 60 percent of the rural population lives on less than two rupees a day. The wax is sold in Kathmandu to the artisans who use it in the lost-wax process of casting statues.

Two trips are necessary to bring all the honey back to the village. Hands on their temples, the men grip the straps supporting the heavy *dokkos*. The loads pull so much that the hunters feel as if their heads are being torn off. Beads of sweat glisten on their faces. The day is hot and humid. With a long whistle like a sigh, Amarzang proposes to stop. "No," replies Mani Lal, "we will stop up there on the ridge to drink the air."

Half an hour later, they reach the shade of a fir tree on the ridge. A breath of air stirs the leaves. With a grimace of pain, their heads straining against the weight of their burdens, the hunters slip the belts off their foreheads and place the *dokkos* on the stone wall where, for hundreds of years, porters have rested their loads. They light up cigarettes and, without saying a word, look at their valley stretched out before them. Towards the south, the ridges are blurred by a mist of rain. Heavy clouds illuminated by a ballet of lightning warn that the monsoon is approaching. "The rain will soon come," says Mani Lal. "It's time to return to our village and plant the millet."

Mani Lal has decided that this autumn will be the last time that he will hunt the honey. With him, this timeless quest will end, for he has no successor.

On the cover: Mani Lal, with the tools of his trade, two bamboo poles, and Sri Lal, with the family's percussion musket, pose against the forest background.

1. Barta, the eighty-three-year-old father of Mani Lal and Sri Lal, passed down the lore of the honey hunt to Mani Lal, his eldest son, after Barta was blinded by a bee sting thirty-five years ago.

2. & 3. The land of the Gurungs lies along the southern slopes of the Himalayas, in central Nepal. With the demand for land near the villages outstripping the availability, families settle permanently in forest huts that were once the summertime shelters of the buffalo herders.

4. & 5. The Gurungs have long been hunters and soldiers. Midge, the best hunter of his village, poses with his parents. Behind, stretched out to dry on a bamboo frame, is the skin of a tahr, a Himalayan wild goat. Karma Bahadur and Chitra Bahadur, veterans of Gurkha regiments serving in the Second World War, proudly show their medals.

6. & 7. Men Bahadur, who has sole charge of the ladder, closes the file of hunters. At times he must walk sideways to accommodate the 160-foot-long ladder on the narrow forest trails.

8, 9, & 10. The hunters make the ladder and all their ropes from the cortex of mountain bamboo. On arriving at the top of the cliff, Men Bahadur unrolls the ladder over the precipice and secures it to a tree. His job is then to move the ladder as Mani Lal commands.

11. & 12. Krishna, wrapped in his bokku, a felted woolen cape, watches Mani Lal descend the cliff.

13. Mani Lal moves from one bees' colony to the next by leaping across the cliff face on the ladder. The curve of a nest, covered with bees, is visible below him.

14. Mani Lal's brown-hooded figure at the yellow comb of the nest are dwarfed by the 425-foot-high cliff known as Samser Bir. Eric, in blue, rappelled down alongside Mani Lal to take close-up shots of the hunter in action.

15. Smoke from a bundle of burning leaves, lowered from the top of the cliff, disperses the bees, and the golden crescent shape of the colony is revealed. The white specks around the nest are the bees flying in an angry swarm. Mani Lal, obscured by the cloud of smoke, waits for the bees to depart.

16. & 17. Wedging the basket under the hive with one bamboo pole, Mani Lal uses the second bamboo to scoop out the honeycomb stuck to the rock face.

18. to 21. Mani Lal breaks the mass of nursery, or brood, cells away. Attached to a rope, the crescent swings like a pendulum and Mani Lal pushes it away from the ladder. The nursery cells are lowered to the base of the cliff. Mani Lal pushes the basket into place under the honeycomb before starting to remove the honey.

22. & 23. As the basket filled with honeycomb is lowered down to the hunters, Mani Lal relaxes with a cigarette and sizes up the next colony.

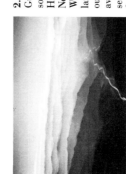

41. & 42. The percussion muskets used by the hunters were made by the blacksmiths of the valley. Passed down from generation to generation, the guns are sometimes 100 years old.

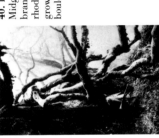

43. to 45. The men hunt in the jungle for days at a time, sleeping in the open and rising at dawn to look for fresh traces, such as these droppings of the musk deer.

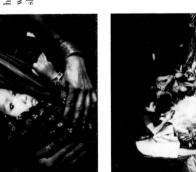

46. & 47. Midge carries a wolf that he shot and killed. Wolves are hunted because they attack the villagers' herds of sheep and buffalo. Midge examines the skin of a *ghoral* left to dry.

36. & 37. In April, the rhododendrons are in full bloom. The hunters walk through forests of red and white flowers on the trail of wolves, *ghoral*—a small antelope—*tahr*, and musk deer. Behind the clouds, the hunters glimpse the peaks of the Himalayas.

38. & 39. Midge searches for fresh animal tracks in the alpine grasses. The hunters walk barefoot; the soles of their feet grip the rocks securely, and their strong toes prevent them from slipping in the mud.
In the jungle the leeches feast on the hunters' feet and ankles, their bites leaving trickles of blood.

40. In the misty forest, Midge walks under the branches of an enormous rhododendron that has grown over the edge of a boulder.

30. & 31. The women and children stay in the village while the men go hunting.
These three friends were about to leave for the three-day walk to the nearest Gurkha army office to collect their war-widows' pensions.

32. & 33. On the verandah of his mud-brick house, Mani Lal melts the wax before filtering out the impurities. His wife looks on from the doorway. A woman neighbor relaxes in the afternoon with a water pipe of tobacco.

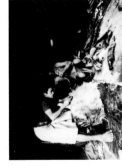

34. & 35. A little Gurung girl, cradled in her mother's arms, watches two hunters skinning a *tahr*.

24. & 25. Suspended on his ladder in a 160-foot void, Mani Lal breaks the nursery cells away from the honeycomb.

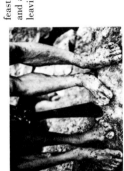
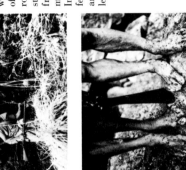

26. & 27. Akam takes the block of nursery cells as soon as it reaches the bottom of the cliff. Sri Lal is only able to carry the six-foot-wide crescent back to camp by folding it in two.

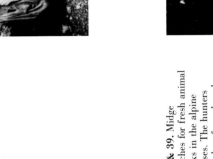

28. & 29. Mani Lal's face reflects a day of harvesting the nests.
The terraced rice fields of his village are golden in the light of the setting sun. The hunters do not have sufficient land to support their families, and the honey is traded for grain to make up for the shortfall.

66. & 67. The family of hunters poses: from left to right (back row), Akam, Nanda Lal, Bal Bahadur, Sri Lal, Amarzang, and Krishna; (front row) Men Bahadur, Mani Lal, and Purké. During a hunt, all that they have—food, honey, cigarettes, and the hookah—is shared. Nanda Lal takes a turn at smoking the water pipe while Men Bahadur loads his gun.

68. & 69. At the end of a day's work on the cliffs, Men Bahadur's face is graven with fatigue. Sri Lal falls asleep with the containers of honey beside him.

70. & 71. Lost in thought, Sri Lal stares past the camera. From a lifetime of walking barefoot, the soles of his feet are as tough and worn as old leather.

60. & 61. The hunter fastens a cord through the mass of nursery cells before he breaks it away. When the edge of the crescent is white, Mani Lal breaks off a piece to place in the protective charms worn by his family.

62. & 63. A *bokku* frames Sri Lal's face. He places his hand on the golden crescent of wax.

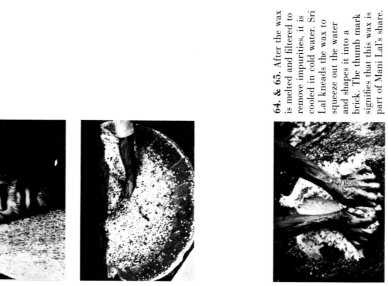

64. & 65. After the wax is melted and filtered to remove impurities, it is cooled in cold water. Sri Lal kneads the wax to squeeze out the water and shapes it into a brick. The thumb mark signifies that this wax is part of Mani Lal's share.

55. & 56. On an overhanging cliff, Akam and Krishna hold the ladder against the rock face to bring Mani Lal closer to the colony.

57. & 58. Some of the bees' nests are almost as big as Mani Lal. This colony, six feet wide and four feet long, appears brown because of the thousands of bees covering the surface. Thick smoke from a fire lit at the base of the cliff disperses the bees into an angry swarm that will attack any moving creature.

59. Mani Lal works at a nest with the same determination and strength that keep him on the ladder for up to four hours at a time.

48. A hunter brings a *ghoral* back to camp.

49. The honey hunters prepare for their campaign: the ladder is thoroughly checked, and the wooden rungs are secured with new bamboo twine.

50. Once Mani Lal is on the cliff, his life depends on the ladder's strength.

51. to 54. Mani Lal secures himself to the ladder with a bamboo cord, leaving his hands and feet free to work. Every limb of his agile body is in motion: one foot grips a rung for balance, the other keeps the bamboo pole—and the basket it holds under the nest—in place. With the second pole, Mani Lal cuts into the honeycomb.

ABOUT THE AUTHORS

Eric Valli and Diane Summers have lived in Nepal for several years and speak the language of the country fluently. They have traveled extensively over the Himalayas, seeking to record the intimate aspects of people's lives. For eight months, Valli and Summers shared the lives of the hunters in the forest. The close bonds of friendship that formed allowed them to present an insider's view of the lives of these remarkable people. The photographs won the 1988 World Press prize for nature, and a selection appears in the November 1988 issue of *National Geographic*. Although the story of the honey hunting goes back to time immemorial, it has never before been photographed.

Their work focusing on different facets of Nepalese culture and nature has appeared in numerous publications, including *GEO* in France and Germany, *Smithsonian*, and *Le Figaro*. *Honey Hunters of Nepal* is their fourth book on that country.

82. & 83. Amarzang relaxes. Sometimes the hunters smoke cigarettes to ward away the stinging bees.
Akam's, Amarzang's, and Men Bahadur's faces are swollen from bee stings.

85. Sri Lal rests with his grandfather's gun at the end of the hunt. Behind him, the first clouds of the monsoon fill the gorges.

77. & 78. Protected in their *boktas* from the angry bees, the villagers encircle the first basket of honeycomb lowered from the nest.
Nanda Lal quickly scoops the contents into a bamboo filter, because Mani Lal is waiting on the ladder for the basket to be sent up for the next load.

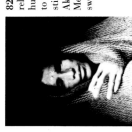

79. & 80. A bee crawls over the lower section of the nest, which contains the nursery cells, each measuring a little over a quarter of an inch across. With an average length of four-fifths of an inch, *Apis laboriosa* is the largest honeybee in the world. These bees live at altitudes between 3,900 feet and 11,500 feet; it is believed that they are hairier than other honeybees because of the cooler climate.
Sri Lal squeezes the larva cells; the milky liquid, rich in protein, will be cooked with chilis and salt.

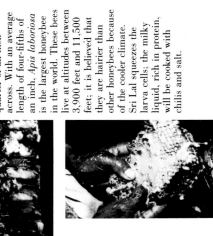
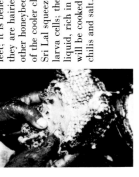

81. In the blue smoke of the fires and among the bees, Mani Lal descends the ladder.

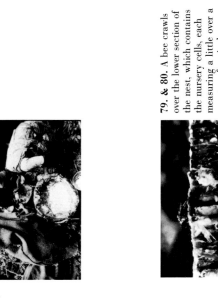

72. Suspended 160 feet above the heads of the hunters, Mani Lal waits for Krishna and Akam to pull the ladder closer to the cliff face. Only the white edge of the first colony remains. Just below are the golden crescents of two other nests that Mani Lal will also cut.

73. Krishna, who has secured the ladder below the overhanging cliff, does not have the safety of a rope and grips the rock face below Mani Lal. Only the pinpricks of the hunters' heads are visible as they filter the honey.

74. Mani Lal thrusts a bamboo pole into the nursery cells.

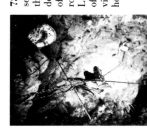

75. & 76. As Mani Lal breaks the honeycomb away from the rock face and into the basket, honey falls like rain into the pans and pots held by villagers. People from the hunters' village have the right to take some of the honey during the harvest in return for contributing to the annual tax.

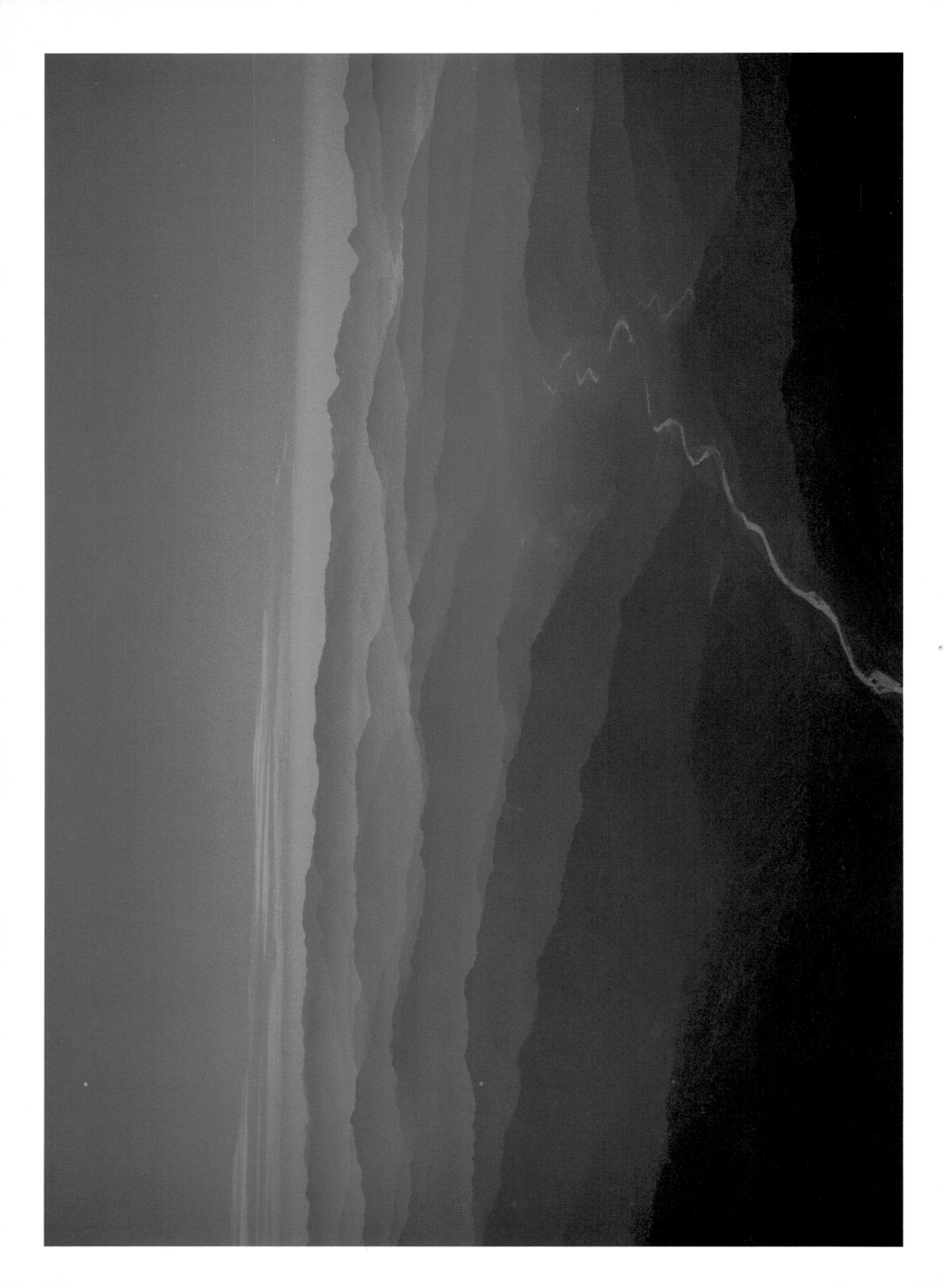

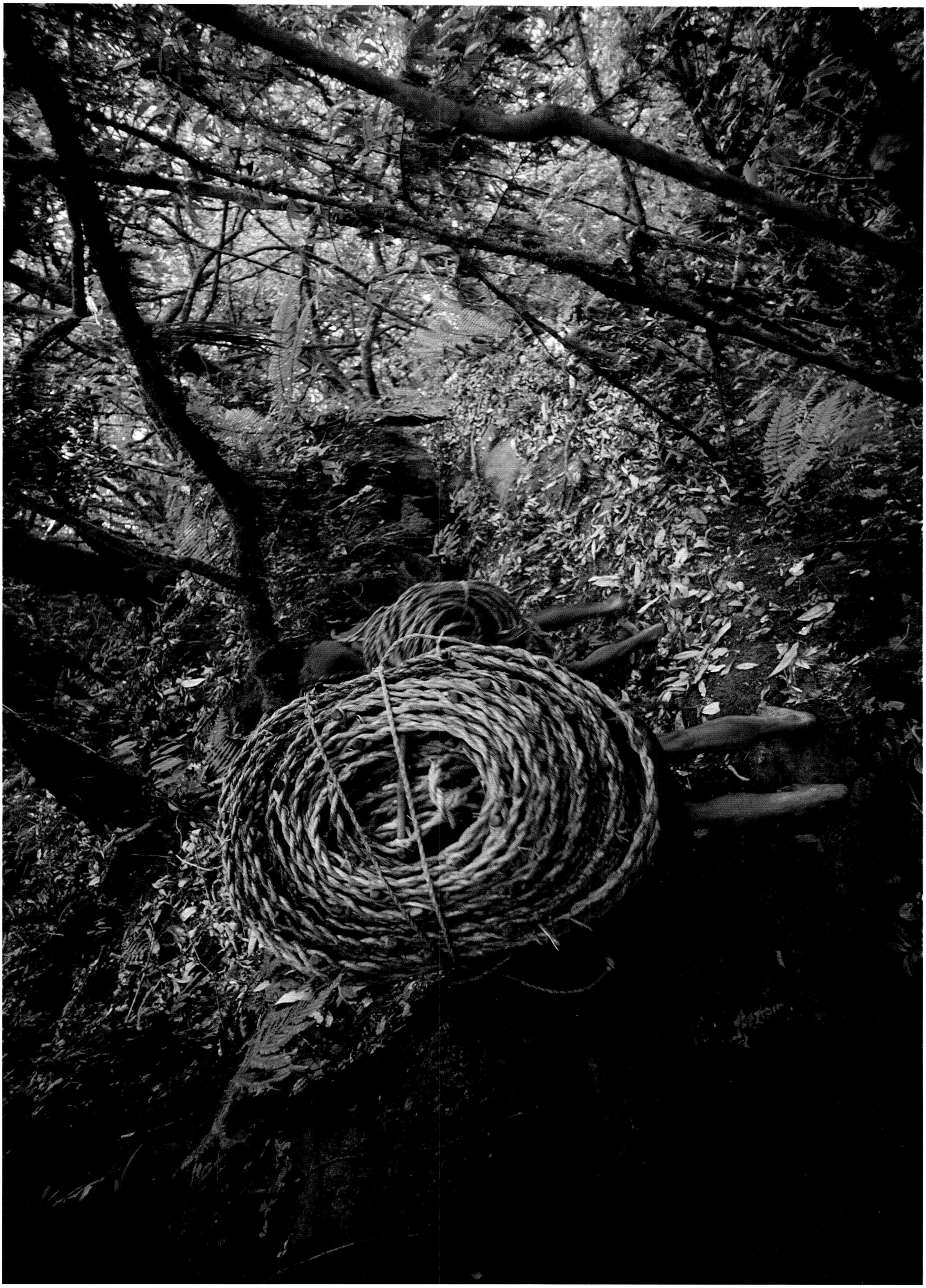